# The Diver

Sandra Woodcock

*Published in association with*
The Basic Skills Agency

Hodder Murray
A MEMBER OF THE HODDER HEADLINE GROUP

Orders: please contact Bookpoint Ltd, 130 Milton Park, Abingdon, Oxon OX14 4SB.
Telephone: (44) 01235 827720. Fax: (44) 01235 400454. Lines are open 9.00–6.00,
Monday to Saturday, with a 24-hour message answering service. Visit our website at
www.hoddereducation.co.uk

First published in 2005 by
Hodder Murray, a member of the Hodder Headline Group
338 Euston Road
London NW1 3BH

Impression number   10 9 8 7 6 5 4 3 2 1
Year                      2010 2009 2008 2007 2006 2005

Cover illustration: Janos Jantner/Beehive Illustration.
Illustrations: Pulsar Studio/Beehive Illustration.
Typeset by Transet Limited, Coventry, England.
Printed in Great Britain by Athenaeum Press Ltd, Gateshead, Tyne & Wear.

A catalogue record for this title is available from the British Library

ISBN-10 0 340 90057 1
ISBN-13 9 780340 900574

# Contents

# 1
# Best Friends

---

Pete and Matt were best friends.
They had been at school together.
They had played football for the same team.
Matt was best man when Pete got married.

They both lived in the same seaside town
in Devon.
They were keen on swimming and diving.
Pete and Matt had been on some
really good trips.
But the best of all was wreck diving.
Nothing beat the thrill of finding a ship
that had lain at the bottom of the sea
for 30, 40, 100 years or even longer.

Pete had done more diving than Matt.
He knew lots of divers.
For weeks he had been talking about
a trip to see a mate in Scotland –
another diver called Joe.

Pete told Matt about his special trip.
'Joe knows this fantastic place.
There's a wreck.
Not many people know about it.
It's a submarine. Went down in the 1940s.'

Matt was a bit jealous.
But he looked at the map with Pete.
They talked about diving in Scottish waters
instead of the English Channel.
Pete told him a bit about the wreck.
It would be so good to dive down
to something that few other divers had seen.

Matt got used to the idea
that Pete was going and he wasn't.
Then everything changed.

# 2
# A Lucky Break

Matt was reading the paper
when Pete called in to see him.
'Hey, mate!  How's things?' said Pete.


'Hi Pete! I'm OK.
How about you? Ready for your dive?'

'Well… things have changed.
Zac's got to go into hospital again.'

Pete's little boy, Zac,
was having a bad time.
Matt didn't know what to say.
It was hard to talk about this…
even with a best friend.

'It's OK, he's not too bad.
But it means my trip to Scotland is off.
That's why I'm here.'

Matt looked puzzled.

'It's your big chance, mate,' said Pete.
'I want you to go instead of me.'

'But I can't,' Matt said. 'I mean…
I don't know Joe.
I don't know that part of Scotland.'

But Pete would not take no for an answer.

'Come on mate, you'll be fine.
Joe's a good man.
He's a first-class diver.
He'll look after you.
Everything's set up.
I've got a room booked
at the pub in the village.
Joe's booked time off work.
Why waste it?
Anyway, if you go and it's good,
you can take me some other time.
Come on Matt, do it for me.
It's your lucky break!'

# 3
# Scotland

---

Matt thought about it.
It was a long drive to Scotland.
But he could stay one night in Newcastle
at his brother's house.
It would give them a chance to catch up
on family news.

Matt made up his mind.
He would go to Scotland.

So he set off for his brother's house.
It was a fine day and the journey
wasn't too bad.
His brother was pleased to see him.
They had a good night in the pub.

Later the next day Matt set off for Scotland.
Joe was going to meet him there.
All he had to do was find the little village
and the pub.

But the village was in a lonely part
of Scotland.
There was nothing for miles around.
Matt got lost three times.
He had to keep stopping to look at the map.

There was no one to ask.
It was getting dark.
He was getting more bad-tempered.
At last he found the old coast road
that took him into the village.

The pub where he had to stay
was close to the rocky shore.
It was past midnight but Matt was glad to see
that the lights were on.

There was only one person inside the pub
– the landlord.
'You must be Matt,' he said.
'We had your mate on the phone
about the change of plan.
Come on, I'll show you the room.'

The landlord was keen to get to bed
but Matt wanted some fresh air.
'I'll just go out for five minutes,' he said.

Outside there was a sea mist.
The night was black.
There was no moon and no stars.
Matt walked a little way
along the rocky shore.
Fingers of mist touched his face and neck.
The wind pulled at his hair and his coat.
He was being pulled towards the sea.
There was something about this place
he didn't like.
It seemed like the edge of the world.

Then suddenly a dark shape
came out of the mist.
Matt cried out.
His ankle turned on a rock
and he fell to the ground.

# 4
# Meeting Joe
---

Matt looked up.
The dark shape was above him.
It was a man.
He held out his hand and helped Matt up.

'Are you here for the wreck?' he asked.

'Joe! Thank goodness!' said Matt.
He shook the man's hand,
laughing with relief,
angry with himself for feeling afraid.

'We dive tomorrow morning.
I'll see you here at first light.
Be ready.'

He turned away.
The mist closed over him
before Matt could call out 'Wait!'

Matt limped back to the pub.
He could not believe it.
How could anybody be so rude?
Joe was a very strange man.
Where was he staying?
And why hadn't he stopped for a proper talk?
He didn't seem like the sort of man
Pete would get on with.

Matt began to think badly of Pete.
Why had he talked him into this crazy trip?
He would ring him up and tell him
just what he thought about Joe.

He reached for his mobile but it wasn't there.
'Damn. I must have dropped it
when I fell,' he said.
He would find it in the morning.
No one was likely to pick it up out there.

# 5
# The Dive

_____

Matt woke early.
It was still dark,
but it would soon be first light.
Time to meet Joe.
He pulled on his wetsuit
and took the rest of his gear outside.
He set off to look for his mobile
on the rocky shore.
Suddenly Joe was there.
It was just like the night before.
One minute he wasn't there,
the next minute he was right beside Matt.
Matt jumped. 'You gave me a scare,' he said.

Joe was looking out to sea.
'Time to go down,' he said.
'Get your gear.'

When they were both ready,
Joe walked into the sea
and began to wade out.

No boat, thought Matt.
It must get deep quite soon.
He went in after Joe.

Under the water he found himself
on a wide shelf of rock.
He could see that it was like the top
of an underground cliff.
As they swam away from it,
the water suddenly became deep.

Matt followed Joe deeper and deeper.
He was surprised how much he could see.
On dives in the English Channel
you were lucky to see 3 metres ahead.
Here they could see 10, even 15 metres.
And there was so much to see –
more underground cliffs and rock faces.

The rocks were covered
with the bright colours of sea plants.
They were like underwater hanging gardens.

There were fish and other sea creatures
Matt had never seen before.

They went deeper still. Matt began to worry.
It was dangerous to go too deep.
He had never been deeper than 50 metres.
They had already gone past that.
But Joe was waving him on.
The water was not so clear now.
It was like an underwater fog.

Then he saw it.
The submarine wreck
standing tall in the flat seabed.

It was fantastic.
It was covered with sea plants
and was a magnet for all kinds of fish.
But there seemed to be little damage.
It was a complete submarine.

Matt swam close up to look at the gun.
He looked around for Joe
but he was nowhere to be seen.
He must have gone inside the wreck.
Matt swam around the sides of the wreck
looking for an entrance.

Then he saw a door open in the side
and caught a glimpse of Joe.
But there was something else…
As he swam into the sub he saw a hand –
a skeleton hand.
A skull bobbed in the water
as if nodding to him.
He saw more skeletons,
more bony arms and fingers,
more skulls with black empty eye-holes
and grinning teeth.
They seemed to be pulling him in,
sucking him into their coffin in the sea.

Matt came to his senses.
He kicked away and tried to swim
out of the door.
But something was wrong.
Something was wrong with his air supply.
In mad panic he kicked and pushed.
But there was no hope. He had come too far.
He had been underwater too long.
He had no air left.
A bony finger seemed to beckon him in
to share the watery grave.

# 6

# Messages for Matt

Back in the village,
little Megan Morris was playing
with her brother Jimmy
on the rocky shore outside the pub.

'Tell me that story about the ship
that Grandad told you, Jimmy.'

'I can't,' Jimmy said.
'It's too scary.
It will give you bad dreams.'

'OK, then. I won't show you my treasure
that I just found.'

Jimmy looked bored, so Megan began to shout.
'Tell me it! Tell me! Tell me!'

'OK then, and if you get scared
it's your own fault.'

So Jimmy told Megan the story he heard
from his grandad.

Many years ago a submarine was lost
at the bottom of the sea.
All the men were trapped inside
where they died.
People living in the village sometimes hear
the screams of the dying sailors.
The old men say that every so often,
a ghost from the wreck comes up to the shore
looking for help to rescue them all.

'So you watch out little Megan
or a ghost may come and grab you
and suck you down to the bottom of the sea
and never let you go.'
And Jimmy grabbed his little sister
to make her scream.

'Now show me your treasure,' he said.

Megan took something out of her bag.

'Megan Morris! That's a mobile phone
you've got there.
You must hand that in.
And it's flashing – it's got a message.'

They took the mobile to their grandad.
He was having a drink in the pub.
He read out the text message.
It was from someone called Pete.

'Hey Matt – this dive is jinxed.
Now Joe can't make it.
Sorry if you've had a wasted journey. Pete'

'Now that makes sense,' said the pub landlord.
'I have just taken a phone message for Matt
from a chap called Joe.'

The message Joe had left said:
'Sorry to mess you around, Matt.
My car broke down in Glasgow.
I'll be with you as soon as it's fixed –
hopefully in a day or two.'

'Now all we have to do,' said the landlord,
'is find Matt to let him know.'